ST JOHN

TRAVEL GUIDE

2024-2025

Experience an Unforgettable Tourist Adventure in the USVI.

Suitable for Budget and Luxury Travelers

Copyright © 2024 [Thomas Cross]

Table of Contents

My Journey in St. John

From the moment I stepped off the ferry onto the shores of St. John, I knew I was in for an adventure like no other. The salty breeze, the swaying palm trees, and the vibrant colors of Cruz Bay immediately enveloped me in a warm embrace. It felt like the island itself was welcoming me with open arms.

Armed with this comprehensive travel guide, I navigated the charming streets of Cruz Bay with ease. My first stop was a quaint café recommended in the book, where the aroma of freshly brewed coffee mingled with the scent of the ocean. The barista, a friendly local, chatted with me about the best hiking trails, and I felt an immediate connection to the island's community.

With a spring in my step, I set off to explore the Virgin Islands National Park. The guide's detailed maps and trail descriptions made it effortless to find my way. Hiking through lush greenery, I stumbled upon breathtaking vistas and hidden beaches that seemed untouched by time. Each turn in the trail revealed a new wonder, and I felt like an intrepid explorer uncovering nature's secrets.

Lunchtime called for a culinary adventure, and the guide did not disappoint. I found myself at a local eatery savoring mouthwatering conch fritters and sipping on a refreshing tamarind juice. The section on local specialties had piqued my curiosity, and every bite was a delightful discovery of St. John's rich culinary heritage.

In the afternoon, I wandered through the historic ruins of Annaberg Plantation, immersing myself in the island's storied past. The guide's insightful historical anecdotes brought the site to life, and I could almost hear the echoes of history in the whispering winds.

As the sun began to set, I headed to Trunk Bay, one of the island's most famous beaches. The guide's tips on the best times to visit ensured I arrived just as the sky transformed into a canvas of oranges and pinks. I dipped my toes into the crystal-clear waters and felt an overwhelming sense of tranquility. It was a moment of pure bliss, perfectly captured by the beauty of St. John.

My journey was rounded off with a visit to a local market, where I picked up handcrafted souvenirs to remind me of this magical place. The guide's recommendations led me to unique finds that I'll treasure forever.

Reflecting on my adventure, I realized that this travel guide was more than just a book—it was a trusted companion that enriched every moment of my trip. It provided not only practical information but also a heartfelt connection to the island's soul.

If you're planning a trip to St. John, this guide is your ticket to an unforgettable experience. Let it lead you to hidden gems, culinary delights, and cultural treasures. St. John is waiting to enchant you, and this guide is the key to unlocking its wonders. Trust me, your island adventure awaits.

Stephanie Jackson. N

Introduction to St. John

Overview and Historical Significance of St. John

Welcome to St. John, the enchanting jewel of the U.S. Virgin Islands! Picture yourself stepping onto an island where the past and present blend seamlessly, where every breeze carries whispers of history, and every sunset feels like a painting come to life. St. John isn't just a tropical paradise—it's a place where stories unfold with every step you take.

Let's take a stroll back in time, shall we? Originally inhabited by the Arawak and Carib peoples, St. John has a history as rich and diverse as its stunning landscapes. In 1718, the Danish West India and Guinea Company claimed the island, kickstarting a period of colonization that would shape its future. The Danes established sugar plantations, and with them came the dark era of slavery. The island's lush hillsides still hold the ruins of these plantations, standing as silent reminders of a tumultuous past.

But St. John's history isn't all about hardship. In 1733, the enslaved African population orchestrated one of the first significant slave revolts in the New World. Their bravery is etched into the island's soul, and their legacy is celebrated and remembered, infusing St. John with a spirit of resilience and freedom.

Fast forward to the 20th century, and you'll find a turning point that transformed St. John into the paradise we know today. In 1956, a generous donation of land by Laurence Rockefeller led to the establishment of the Virgin Islands National Park, protecting over twothirds of the island from development. This move preserved St. John's natural beauty, making it a haven for nature lovers and adventure seekers alike.

Today, St. John is a blend of pristine beaches, verdant hills, and a lively, welcoming community. Cruz Bay, the island's bustling hub, is where modern conveniences meet laidback island vibes. It's the perfect place to start your adventure, with its vibrant shops, cozy cafes, and friendly locals ready to share a tale or two.

As you explore, you'll find that St. John is more than just a pretty face. It's an island with a story, one that invites you to discover its layers and fall in love with its charm. Whether you're snorkeling in the azure waters of Trunk Bay, hiking through the lush trails of the national park, or simply soaking up the sun on a secluded beach, you're not just a visitor—you're part of St. John's ongoing narrative.

So, pack your bags, bring your curiosity, and get ready to write your own chapter in the captivating history of St. John. And don't forget to have a laugh or two along the way—after all, every great story needs a bit of humor!

Modern St. John

Welcome to modern St. John, where the island's vibrant present is as compelling as its storied past. Imagine an idyllic paradise where stunning natural beauty coexists harmoniously with lively island culture. Yes, St. John is the epitome of island charm with a contemporary twist, ready to offer you a slice of heaven wrapped in a warm, tropical embrace.

As you step off the ferry at Cruz Bay, the island's energetic heartbeat, you'll feel the welcome embrace of a community that knows how to blend laidback living with a touch of modernity. Picture this: quaint streets lined with eclectic boutiques, art galleries showcasing local talent, and an array of eateries serving up everything from mouthwatering Caribbean cuisine to international delights. This isn't just any island; it's a haven for foodies and shopaholics alike.

While strolling through Cruz Bay, don't be surprised if you find yourself striking up a conversation with a local who seems to know everyone and everything about the island. Their stories are as rich and flavorful as the dishes served at the local food joints. Speaking of food, have you tried a paté from a street vendor? It's a culinary experience as delightful as discovering a secret ingredient in your favorite dish—unexpected and absolutely satisfying.

Modern St. John is not just about leisure and luxury; it's about living sustainably and respecting the island's natural bounty. The community here takes great pride in preserving their pristine environment. You'll find ecofriendly accommodations and activities that promote conservation, like reefsafe sunscreen mandates and sustainable fishing practices. It's a place where you can enjoy the luxuries of modern living without leaving a heavy footprint.

Adventure enthusiasts will find their paradise here. From the breathtaking hikes through Virgin Islands National Park to the exhilarating water sports in the turquoise waters, St. John offers activities that will get your adrenaline pumping. Try paddleboarding at Maho Bay or exploring the underwater trail at Trunk Bay. And if you're feeling particularly adventurous, a night kayak tour through the bioluminescent bays will make you believe in magic.

But don't worry, there's plenty of room for relaxation. Imagine yourself lounging on a pristine beach, the only sounds being the gentle lapping of waves and the rustling of palm fronds. Or perhaps you'd prefer a luxurious spa day, where every massage stroke feels like a lullaby sung by the island itself.

Modern St. John is a place where every day feels like a celebration. Whether it's a local festival, a sunset sail, or simply enjoying a cocktail with friends as the sun dips below the horizon, there's a joy here that's infectious. It's an island where you can let your hair down, kick off your shoes, and embrace the spirit of 'island time.'

So, come and experience the modern marvel that is St. John. It's not just a destination; it's a feeling, a story, a dream come true. And trust us, once you've experienced the charm of modern St. John, you'll never want to leave.

Planning Your Trip

Best Time to Visit

Choosing the best time to visit St. John is like picking the perfect slice of pie—every season has its own delicious charm, and you can't really go wrong. But let's slice this island paradise into its seasonal flavors, so you can find the time that best suits your travel appetite.

Winter (December to February)

Ah, winter—when the rest of the world is bundled up in woolly sweaters, you could be basking in the balmy 70s and 80s on a pristine beach. This is high season in St. John, with tourists flocking to escape the cold. Think of it as the island's social butterfly season. The beaches are buzzing, the bars are hopping, and there's a festive spirit in the air. It's the perfect time to mingle, make new friends, and enjoy the vibrant nightlife. Just remember to book your accommodations well in advance and be prepared for slightly higher prices.

Spring (March to May)

Spring on St. John is like finding the sweet spot in a hammock—utterly delightful and just right. The weather is still warm and inviting, but the winter crowds have started to thin out. This is a great time for those who want a bit of buzz without the hustle and bustle of peak season. The island's flora is in full bloom, making hikes through Virgin Islands National Park a colorful and fragrant experience. Plus, the waters are perfect for snorkeling and diving, with excellent visibility and a vibrant marine life show just beneath the surface.

Summer (June to August)

Summer is St. John's warm embrace, with temperatures climbing into the 80s and 90s. It's the low season, which means fewer tourists and more room to stretch out on those beautiful beaches. Prices for accommodations drop, and you can often find great deals. The downside? It's also hurricane season, so there's a chance of some wet and windy weather. But don't let that scare you away—just keep an eye on the weather forecast and enjoy the tranquility that comes with having a slice of paradise almost to yourself.

Fall (September to November)

Fall on St. John is like the island's serene sigh before the holiday rush. The weather is still warm, the summer rains are tapering off, and the hurricane season is winding down. This is a wonderful time to visit if you prefer a quieter, more laidback experience.

The island is lush and green from the summer rains, and the sunsets are particularly stunning. Plus, you can snag some great offseason deals on accommodations and activities.

A Bit of Advice

Whenever you choose to visit, remember to pack your sense of humor along with your sunscreen. Island time is a real thing—things move a little slower, and that's part of the charm. Your restaurant order might take a little longer, but hey, you're in paradise! Relax, sip your drink, and enjoy the view.

So, whether you're escaping the winter blues, chasing spring blossoms, enjoying summer's tranquility, or soaking in fall's serene beauty, St. John is ready to welcome you with open arms and a warm smile. Pack your bags, embrace the island spirit, and get ready for an unforgettable adventure!

Travel Tips

Traveling to St. John is like embarking on an adventure to a tropical paradise, where preparation and a touch of savvy can make your trip even more delightful. Here are some handy travel tips to ensure you have a smooth and enjoyable journey.

1. <u>Book in Advance</u>: St. John is a popular destination, especially during the high season. Make sure to book your flights, accommodations, and car rentals well in advance to secure the best deals and options. Remember, you're not the only one dreaming of island bliss!

2. <u>Travel Insurance</u>: This might sound as exciting as watching paint dry, but trust us, travel insurance is your best friend. Whether it's for medical emergencies, trip cancellations, or unexpected hurricanes, having insurance can save you from potential headaches.

3. <u>Pack Light</u>: You're heading to a laidback island, not a fashion show. Bring light, breathable clothing, swimwear, and comfortable footwear. Think flipflops, not stilettos. And don't forget a hat and sunglasses to protect yourself from the sun.

4. <u>Stay Connected</u>: If you plan to stay connected with the world beyond the island, check with your mobile provider about international roaming rates. Alternatively, consider getting a local SIM card or using WiFi for your communication needs.

5. <u>Cash and Cards</u>: While credit cards are widely accepted, it's always good to have some cash on hand for small purchases, tips, and those quaint local markets. There are ATMs available, but having some U.S. dollars upon arrival can save you time.

6. <u>Transportation</u>: Renting a car, particularly a Jeep, is highly recommended for exploring the island. The terrain can be hilly and rugged, and a sturdy vehicle will make your adventures more comfortable. Just remember to drive on the left side of the road—this isn't the mainland!

7. <u>Respect Nature</u>: St. John is a treasure trove of natural beauty. Help keep it that way by respecting local wildlife, staying on marked trails, and using reefsafe sunscreen to protect the marine life. Leave only footprints, take only memories!

8. <u>Island Time</u>: Embrace the relaxed pace of island life. Things might move a bit slower than you're used to, but that's part of the charm. Take a deep breath, relax, and enjoy the slower pace. After all, you're on vacation!

Packing Essentials

Packing for St. John is all about being prepared for both relaxation and adventure. Here's a list of essentials to ensure you're ready for anything the island throws your way.

1. <u>Sun Protection</u>: Sunscreen (reefsafe, of course), a widebrimmed hat, and sunglasses are a must. The Caribbean sun is strong, and you'll want to enjoy your days without turning into a lobster.

2. <u>Swim Gear</u>: Bring multiple swimsuits, because you'll be spending a lot of time in the water. A rash guard can also be helpful for extra sun protection and snorkeling comfort.

3. <u>Lightweight Clothing</u>: Pack light, breathable fabrics like cotton and linen. Think shorts, tshirts, sundresses,

and coverups. Evenings can be cooler, so a light jacket or sweater is a good idea.

4. Footwear: Flipflops for the beach, sturdy sandals for walking around town, and water shoes if you plan to explore rocky shores and reefs. Hiking shoes are a must if you plan to hit the trails.

5. Reusable Water Bottle: Stay hydrated while reducing plastic waste. Many places on the island have refill stations, making it easy to keep your water bottle topped up.

6. Snorkeling Gear: While you can rent gear on the island, bringing your own mask, snorkel, and fins can save you money and ensure a perfect fit.

7. <u>Bug Spray</u>: Mosquitoes and noseeums (tiny biting insects) can be pesky, especially in the evenings. A good insect repellent will help keep them at bay.

8. <u>First Aid Kit</u>: Basic first aid supplies like bandaids, antiseptic wipes, and any personal medications are good to have on hand. Don't forget seasickness remedies if you're prone to motion sickness.

9. <u>Camera</u>: You'll want to capture the stunning vistas, vibrant marine life, and memorable moments. A waterproof camera or GoPro can be especially handy for underwater adventures.

10. <u>Travel Documents</u>: Passport, travel insurance documents, accommodation confirmations, and a copy of your itinerary. Keep these in a waterproof pouch to protect them from the elements.

Remember, the goal is to pack smart and light, so you can spend less time worrying about your luggage and more time enjoying the island's beauty. Now, go forth and conquer St. John with confidence and style!

Getting to St. John

By Air

Getting to St. John by air is a breeze, albeit with a small twist of island adventure. Since St. John doesn't have its own airport, you'll need to fly into Cyril E. King Airport (STT) on the neighboring island of St. Thomas. But don't worry, this minor detour only adds to the charm and excitement of your journey.

Step 1: Book Your Flight

First things first, book a flight to Cyril E. King Airport (STT), which is wellconnected with major U.S. cities. Airlines such as American Airlines, Delta, United, and JetBlue offer frequent flights, making your tropical dreams just a boarding pass away. Pro tip: keep an eye out for offseason deals and flash sales to save some cash for extra island cocktails.

Step 2: Arrival at St. Thomas

Welcome to St. Thomas! As you step off the plane, the warm Caribbean air greets you like a longlost friend. Breathe it in—your island adventure is just beginning. Collect your luggage, pass through customs, and prepare for the next leg of your journey.

Step 3: Transfer to Red Hook or Charlotte Amalie

Now, you have two main options to get from the airport to the ferry docks: Red Hook or Charlotte Amalie. Red Hook is about a 30minute taxi ride from the airport, while Charlotte Amalie is around 15 minutes away. Taxis are readily available, and you might even share a ride with fellow travelers, turning your taxi into a mini party on wheels. Keep in mind, taxis here charge per person, and rates are fixed, so there's no haggling required.

Step 4: Ferry Ride to St. John

Here's where the fun really begins. Hop on a ferry to St. John and enjoy the scenic 2045 minute ride across the crystalclear waters. Ferries from Red Hook run more frequently, approximately every hour, while those from Charlotte Amalie offer a more leisurely schedule. Either way, you're in for a treat. Grab a seat on the upper deck, feel the breeze in your hair, and let the anticipation build. You're almost there!

Step 5: Arrival in Cruz Bay, St. John

Touchdown! Well, sort of. You'll dock at Cruz Bay, the vibrant heart of St. John. As you disembark, the lively atmosphere immediately envelops you. The first thing you'll notice is the island's undeniable charm— colorful buildings, friendly locals, and the promise of adventure at every corner. From here, it's a short walk or taxi ride to your accommodations.

A Few Tips for Smooth Sailing (or Flying)

- Travel Light: With multiple transfers, keeping your luggage manageable will make your journey more comfortable.

- Cash is King: Have some cash handy for taxi fares and tips. While many places accept cards, cash is often preferred for smaller transactions.
- Island Time: Embrace the slower pace. Delays can happen, but hey, you're on island time now. Relax and go with the flow.

Flying to St. John may require an extra step, but it's all part of the adventure. The stunning vistas and welcoming vibe that await you are well worth the journey. So pack your bags, board that plane, and get ready for an unforgettable island experience!

By Ferry

Traveling to St. John by ferry is like embarking on a mini adventure before your main island escapade. It's a journey that promises stunning views, a taste of local flavor, and a dash of excitement. Let's dive into the details of how to get to this paradise by ferry.

Step 1: Arriving in St. Thomas

First, you'll land at Cyril E. King Airport (STT) on St. Thomas. Once you've navigated through baggage claim and customs, you're ready for the next leg of your journey. Grab a taxi to either the Red Hook Ferry Terminal or the Charlotte Amalie Ferry Terminal.

Red Hook: Located on the eastern tip of St. Thomas, it's about a 30minute taxi ride from the airport.

Charlotte Amalie: Closer to the airport, it's roughly a 15minute ride.

Both options are convenient, but Red Hook offers more frequent ferry services to St. John.

Step 2: Choosing Your Ferry

Here's where the fun begins. The ferry ride is not just a means to an end but a scenic experience that sets the tone for your island getaway. Ferries from Red Hook to Cruz Bay, St. John, run approximately every hour from early morning until midnight. The ride takes about 20 minutes and costs around $7 for adults and $1 for children (plus a small fee for luggage).

From Charlotte Amalie, ferries run less frequently, with a longer ride of about 45 minutes, but it's a direct route through picturesque waters. This option costs a bit more, around $13 for adults and $3 for children, with a similar luggage fee.

Step 3: Enjoy the Ride

As you board the ferry, grab a seat on the upper deck if you can. Feel the warm Caribbean breeze, snap some photos, and strike up a conversation with fellow travelers. The stunning turquoise waters and the anticipation of what lies ahead make this part of the journey truly special. Don't be surprised if you spot a dolphin or two frolicking alongside the ferry.

Step 4: Arriving in Cruz Bay, St. John

When the ferry docks at Cruz Bay, you'll be greeted by the charming, bustling harbor town. The first thing you'll notice is the vibrant atmosphere—locals mingling with tourists, shops and restaurants lining the streets, and the undeniable feeling that you've arrived somewhere extraordinary. Whether you're heading straight to your hotel or eager to explore, Cruz Bay's welcoming vibe sets the perfect tone for your stay.

Tips for a Smooth Ferry Ride

- Timing is Everything: Check the ferry schedules in advance, especially if you're arriving late or traveling during offpeak hours.
- Pack Smart: Keep essentials like water, sunscreen, and a hat in your carryon. You'll appreciate having them handy during the ferry ride.
- Cash is Handy: While most places accept cards, having some cash for taxi fares and small purchases makes life easier.
- Embrace Island Time: Ferry schedules can be a bit fluid, so adopt the island's relaxed pace and enjoy the journey.

Traveling by ferry to St. John is more than just a way to get from point A to point B. It's the beginning of your island adventure, offering a sneak peek at the beauty and charm that await you. So sit back, relax, and let the magic of the Caribbean Sea carry you to paradise!

Getting Around St. John

Public Transportation

Navigating St. John with public transportation is like embarking on a whimsical island adventure. The island may be small, but it offers several ways to get around that add to its charm and character. Whether you're hopping on a safari bus or catching a local taxi, here's everything you need to know about public transportation in St. John.

Safari Buses: The Local Experience

Riding a safari bus is perhaps the most authentic way to experience St. John like a local. These openair vehicles, converted from trucks, are a staple of island life. Picture this: you're cruising along the scenic roads with the wind in your hair, surrounded by fellow adventurers and locals alike, all while enjoying panoramic views of the lush landscape.

Routes and Fares: Safari buses primarily run between Cruz Bay and Coral Bay, stopping at various points of interest along the way. The fare is incredibly reasonable, typically around $1$3 per ride. It's a hoponhopoff experience, so you can explore at your own pace.

Tips for Riding: Bring exact change for the fare, as drivers often don't have much change. And don't forget to hold on to your hat—literally! The openair ride can get breezy.

Taxis: Convenience with a View

Taxis on St. John are plentiful and provide a convenient way to get around, especially if you're traveling with luggage or prefer doortodoor service. Unlike traditional metered taxis, fares on the island are set and posted, making it easy to know what you'll pay upfront.

Shared Taxis: Most taxis operate as shared rides, meaning you might find yourself in the company of other tourists heading in the same direction. This can be a great way to meet new people and share travel tips.

Rates and Tips: Rates vary depending on the distance and number of passengers. Expect to pay around $6$15 per person for a trip from Cruz Bay to popular spots like Trunk Bay or Coral Bay. It's customary to tip your driver, especially if they've shared some local knowledge or helped with your bags.

Vitran Buses: The BudgetFriendly Option

For the budgetconscious traveler, the Vitran bus service offers an affordable way to traverse the island. These buses run less frequently than safari buses and taxis but cover the main routes between Cruz Bay, Coral Bay, and other key locations.

Schedules and Fares: The fare is a steal at just $1 per ride. However, the schedules can be a bit erratic, so it's wise to plan ahead and check the latest timetable. Patience is key—this is island time, after all.

Riding Tips: Vitran buses are a great option if you're not in a rush and want to save money. Bring a book or just enjoy the view as you wait for the next bus.

Public transportation on St. John is an adventure in itself. Embrace the laidback island vibe and go with the flow. If you find yourself waiting a bit longer than expected for a ride, remember—you're on vacation! Use the extra time to take in the stunning scenery or strike up a conversation with a local.

A piece of sage advice: always carry a bottle of water and some snacks. The tropical heat can be relentless, and you don't want to be caught thirsty or hungry while waiting for your ride.

Exploring St. John via public transportation is an experience filled with character and local flavor. So hop on a safari bus, catch a taxi, or take the Vitran bus, and enjoy every moment of your island journey. The adventure begins the moment you step on board!

Walking and Hiking

Exploring St. John on foot is a delightful way to immerse yourself in the island's natural beauty and vibrant culture. Whether you're wandering through charming Cruz Bay or trekking through lush forests, walking and hiking offer an intimate glimpse into the island's heart and soul. Lace up your shoes, grab your sense of adventure, and let's hit the trails!

Walking Around Cruz Bay

Cruz Bay is the bustling hub of St. John, and walking is the best way to experience its lively atmosphere. Picture yourself strolling along the colorful streets, where every corner is brimming with local shops, cozy cafes, and vibrant street art. It's a place where the island's laidback vibe meets the buzz of daily life.

- Shopping and Dining: Take a leisurely walk down Mongoose Junction and Wharfside Village, two of the most popular shopping areas. You'll find unique boutiques, artisanal crafts, and mouthwatering eateries. Stop by a local bakery for a fresh pastry or grab a refreshing drink at a beachside bar.
- Historical Sites: Don't miss the Cruz Bay Battery, a historic fortification that offers a peek into the island's past. It's a short walk from the ferry dock and provides a lovely view of the harbor.

Hiking: The Natural Adventure

If you're a nature lover, St. John's hiking trails are a must. The island is part of the Virgin Islands National Park, which covers twothirds of its area, offering a plethora of trails ranging from easy walks to challenging hikes. Each trail presents an opportunity to discover the island's diverse flora, fauna, and stunning vistas.

Reef Bay Trail: This trail is a favorite among hikers. It's a moderately challenging 3mile descent through the forest, featuring ancient petroglyphs, historic sugar mill ruins, and a refreshing swim at the end. The journey back up is a bit strenuous, but the experience is well worth it.

Ram Head Trail: For breathtaking views, Ram Head Trail is your goto. This 2.5mile roundtrip hike starts at Salt Pond Bay and leads to a rocky headland with panoramic views of the Caribbean Sea. The trail is relatively easy, with the wind in your hair and the sound of waves crashing below.

Cinnamon Bay Nature Loop: If you're looking for something shorter and less strenuous, the Cinnamon Bay Nature Loop is perfect. It's an easy walk through a shaded forest, complete with informative signs about the local ecosystem and historical sites along the way.

Tips for a Smooth Hiking Experience

- Stay Hydrated: The tropical sun can be intense, so always carry plenty of water. A reusable water bottle is ideal for keeping hydrated without contributing to plastic waste.

- Wear Appropriate Footwear: Sturdy hiking shoes or sandals are a must. The trails can be rocky and uneven, so proper footwear will keep your feet happy and blisterfree.

- Sun Protection: Sunscreen, a widebrimmed hat, and sunglasses are essential. The last thing you want is to cut your adventure short because of a sunburn.

- Bug Spray: The lush environment means bugs, especially mosquitoes. Pack some insect repellent to keep those pesky critters at bay.
- Respect Nature: Stay on marked trails, take your trash with you, and avoid disturbing wildlife. St. John's natural beauty is a treasure that needs preserving.

Walking and hiking on St. John allow you to connect deeply with the island's essence. Whether you're meandering through Cruz Bay or trekking through the national park, every step reveals new wonders. So, put on your walking shoes, embrace the island's rhythms, and let your adventures unfold one step at a time!

Accommodations

Luxury Hotels in St John

Here are some of the top luxury resorts in St. John, USVI, with detailed descriptions, unique features, hours, price range, location, phone numbers, and a touch of humor and emotion to enhance your luxurious getaway planning. **Please know the time (hours) is susceptible to change so ensure you make enquirements before you try to book**

1. <u>Caneel Bay Resort</u>

Location: North Shore Road, Caneel Bay, St. John, USVI 00830

Phone: (340) 7766111

 Caneel Bay Resort is a legendary luxury resort set within the Virgin Islands National Park. With its stunning beaches and lush surroundings, this resort offers a perfect blend of natural beauty and refined comfort.

Unique Features:

- Seven Pristine Beaches: Access to seven beautiful, private beaches.
- EcoFriendly Design: Emphasis on blending with the natural environment, no televisions in rooms to encourage unplugging.
- Water Activities: Complimentary snorkeling gear, kayaks, and paddleboards.
- Fine Dining: Multiple dining options featuring Caribbean and international cuisine.

Hours:

Checkin: 3:00 PM

Checkout: 12:00 PM

Price Range: $700 $2,500 per night

Staying at Caneel Bay is like living in a dream where the ocean waves serenade you to sleep and the sunrise gently wakes you up. It's a place where luxury meets nature, and every moment feels like a precious escape from reality.

2. **The Westin St. John Resort Villas**

Location: 300B Chocolate Hole, St. John, USVI 00830

Phone: (340) 6938000

 The Westin St. John Resort Villas is a luxurious resort offering spacious villas with all the comforts of home, nestled in a tropical paradise. It's perfect for families or couples seeking both relaxation and adventure.

Unique Features:

- Heavenly Beds: The signature Westin Heavenly Beds for ultimate comfort.
- Spa and Fitness Center: Fullservice spa and stateoftheart fitness center.
- Waterfront Pool: A large pool with a swimup bar and stunning views of Great Cruz Bay.
- Kids Club: Activities and programs for children, ensuring fun for the whole family.

Hours:

Checkin: 4:00 PM

Checkout: 10:00 AM

Price Range: $500 $1,800 per night

The Westin St. John feels like your own private slice of paradise, where every detail is designed to pamper and delight. Whether you're sipping a cocktail by the pool or exploring the island, every moment here feels like a page out of a luxury travel magazine.

3. <u>Gallows Point Resort</u>

Location: 3 AAA Gallows Point Road, Cruz Bay, St. John, USVI 00831

Phone: (340) 7766434

 Gallows Point Resort offers luxurious oceanfront suites with stunning views and modern amenities. Located just a short walk from Cruz Bay, it provides the perfect blend of seclusion and accessibility.

Unique Features:

- Oceanfront Suites: Spacious suites with full kitchens and private balconies overlooking the ocean.
- Infinity Pool: Beautiful pool with panoramic views of the Caribbean Sea.
- OnSite Restaurant: Fine dining at Ocean 362, offering fresh, locally sourced cuisine.
- Private Snorkeling: Direct access to some of the best snorkeling spots on the island.

Hours:

Checkin: 3:00 PM

Checkout: 11:00 AM

Price Range: $450 $1,200 per night

Gallows Point Resort is like finding a hidden gem that sparkles with beauty and tranquility. With the waves crashing just outside your balcony and the vibrant coral reefs beneath, it's a haven for those seeking both luxury and adventure.

4. <u>Estate Lindholm</u>

<u>Location: 6B Estate Lindholm, St. John, USVI 00830</u>

<u>Phone: (340) 7766121</u>

 Estate Lindholm is a charming, boutique resort set on a historic plantation overlooking Cruz Bay. With its intimate setting and personalized service, it offers a unique and luxurious experience.

Unique Features:

- Historic Charm: Set on a restored 18thcentury plantation, offering a rich sense of history.
- Tropical Gardens: Beautifully landscaped gardens filled with native plants and flowers.
- Pool with a View: An infinityedge pool with breathtaking views of Cruz Bay and beyond.
- Complimentary Breakfast: Delicious continental breakfast served daily on the terrace.

Hours:

Checkin: 3:00 PM

Checkout: 11:00 AM

Price Range: $350 $800 per night

Estate Lindholm feels like stepping back in time while enjoying all the modern luxuries. It's a place where history, nature, and comfort merge to create an unforgettable escape. Every morning feels like a fresh start as you enjoy your breakfast with a view that's simply priceless.

5. **Sea Shore Allure**

Location: 271 & 272 Fish Bay Road, Cruz Bay, St. John, USVI 00831

Phone: (340) 7792800

Sea Shore Allure is a luxury boutique resort offering spacious, beautifully appointed condos with stunning views of the Caribbean Sea. It's ideal for travelers seeking privacy and highend amenities.

Unique Features:

- Luxury Condos: Fully equipped condos with gourmet kitchens, large living areas, and private balconies.

- Rooftop Terrace: A rooftop terrace with a hot tub, perfect for relaxing under the stars.

- Beach Access: Easy access to a private beach area.

- Personalized Service: Attentive staff providing personalized service to ensure a memorable stay.

Hours:

Checkin: 3:00 PM

Checkout: 11:00 AM

Price Range: $600 $1,500 per night

Sea Shore Allure is like your personal paradise, where luxury meets the serenity of the sea. With every detail designed to pamper you, it's a place where you can truly unwind and feel the stresses of everyday life melt away.

These luxury resorts in St. John offer exceptional accommodations and amenities, ensuring a memorable and indulgent stay in this tropical paradise. Enjoy planning your luxurious getaway!

MidRange Hotels (B&Bs)

Here are some top midrange hotels in St. John, USVI, with detailed descriptions, unique features, hours, price range, location, phone numbers, and a touch of humor and emotion to enhance your travel planning.

1. **St. John Inn**

Location: 277 Enighed Ln, Cruz Bay, St. John, USVI 00830

Phone: (340) 6938688

 St. John Inn is a charming boutique hotel located in the heart of Cruz Bay. This colorful, familyrun inn offers a cozy and welcoming atmosphere with easy access to local attractions and beaches.

Unique Features:

- Complimentary Breakfast: Enjoy a delightful continental breakfast each morning.
- Outdoor Pool: A refreshing pool area perfect for relaxing after a day of exploring.
- Happy Hour: Daily happy hour with complimentary rum punch.
- Friendly Service: Warm, personalized service from the staff.

Hours:

Checkin: 3:00 PM

Checkout: 11:00 AM

Price Range: $200 $350 per night

Staying at St. John Inn feels like staying with friends who know all the best local secrets. The vibrant colors and friendly vibes make it a joyful retreat where every day starts with a smile and ends with a delicious rum punch toast.

2. Cruz Bay Boutique Hotel

Location: 74 King St, Cruz Bay, St. John, USVI 00830

Phone: (340) 6421702

Cruz Bay Boutique Hotel offers comfortable and stylish accommodations right in the heart of Cruz Bay. This familyowned hotel is known for its excellent location and warm hospitality.

Unique Features:

- Central Location: Just steps away from restaurants, shops, and the ferry dock.
- Modern Amenities: Rooms equipped with air conditioning, flatscreen TVs, and complimentary WiFi.
- Rooftop Terrace: A lovely terrace area for relaxing and enjoying the views.
- Personalized Service: Attentive and friendly staff providing excellent service.

Hours:

Checkin: 3:00 PM

Checkout: 11:00 AM

Price Range: $250 $400 per night

Cruz Bay Boutique Hotel is like the perfect island hideaway, where convenience meets comfort. It's a place where you can step out the door and be in the heart of the action or retreat to your cozy room for a peaceful night's rest.

3. Estate Concordia Preserve

Location: 16371 Concordia, Coral Bay, St. John, USVI 00830

Phone: (340) 7150500

Estate Concordia Preserve is an ecofriendly resort located on the quieter side of the island near Coral Bay. It offers a unique blend of comfort and sustainability, with stunning views of the Caribbean Sea.

Unique Features:

- EcoFriendly Lodging: Solarpowered accommodations designed to minimize environmental impact.
- Scenic Views: Panoramic views of the ocean and surrounding natural beauty.
- OnSite Restaurant: Café Concordia serves delicious, locally sourced meals.
- Nature Trails: Access to hiking trails and outdoor activities.

Hours:

- Checkin: 3:00 PM
- Checkout: 11:00 AM

Price Range: $175 $325 per night

Staying at Estate Concordia Preserve feels like embracing the essence of the island in the most ecoconscious way. It's a place where you can wake up to the sound of birds, breathe in the fresh sea air, and feel good about your carbon footprint.

4. The Inn at Tamarind Court

<u>Location: 4S Contant, Cruz Bay, St. John, USVI 00830</u>

<u>Phone: (340) 7766378</u>

 The Inn at Tamarind Court is a charming and affordable hotel located within walking distance to Cruz Bay's dining, shopping, and entertainment options. It's known for its friendly atmosphere and convenient location.

Unique Features:

- Affordable Comfort: Simple, clean rooms with essential amenities.
- OnSite Restaurant: Tamarind Court Bar & Restaurant serves breakfast, lunch, and dinner.
- Courtyard: A lovely courtyard area for relaxing and socializing.
- Friendly Staff: Warm and welcoming service from the team.

Hours:

- Checking: 3:00 PM
- Checkout: 11:00 AM

Price Range: $150 $250 per night

The Inn at Tamarind Court feels like your favorite neighborhood spot where everyone knows your name. It's a cozy haven where you can relax in the courtyard, enjoy a hearty meal, and feel right at home in the heart of the island.

5. <u>Coconut Coast Villas</u>

<u>Location: 268 Estate Enighed, Cruz Bay, St. John, USVI 00831</u>

<u>Phone: (340) 7766363</u>

 Coconut Coast Villas offers beachfront accommodations with stunning ocean views. This familyowned hotel provides a peaceful and relaxing environment just a short walk from Cruz Bay.

Unique Features:

- Beachfront Location: Direct access to a beautiful beach with crystalclear waters.
- Spacious Villas: Fully equipped villas with kitchens and private balconies.
- Outdoor Pool: A refreshing pool area with ocean views.
- Barbecue Area: Outdoor grills available for guest use.

Hours:

- Checking: 3:00 PM
- Checkout: 11:00 AM

Price Range: $200 $400 per night

Coconut Coast Villas is like finding your own little paradise on the edge of the sea. It's a place where you can wake up to the sound of waves, sip coffee on your balcony, and feel the stresses of everyday life drift away with the tide.

These midrange hotels in St. John offer a comfortable and welcoming stay with a touch of island charm. Enjoy your stay in this beautiful tropical destination!

Cuisine

Local Specialties

St. John's culinary scene is a vibrant tapestry of flavors, a delightful fusion of Caribbean traditions and modern twists. The island's local specialties are a feast for the senses, offering a taste of its rich cultural heritage and bountiful natural resources. Let's embark on a mouthwatering journey through the musttry dishes that make St. John a food lover's paradise.

Conch Fritters: The Island's BiteSized Delight

No trip to St. John is complete without indulging in conch fritters. These goldenbrown morsels are crispy on the outside and tender on the inside, packed with chunks of conch meat, herbs, and spices. Dip them in a tangy sauce, and you've got a snack that's perfect for any time of day. Imagine sitting by the beach, the sun setting in the background, and savoring these delicious bites—pure bliss.

Johnny Cakes: A Caribbean Classic

Johnny cakes are a beloved staple, and for good reason. These fried or baked doughy delights are a versatile treat that can be enjoyed with almost anything. Whether you have them plain, with a drizzle of honey, or paired with savory dishes like saltfish, they're a comforting bite that embodies the island's culinary spirit. They're like the Caribbean's answer to the donut, but way cooler.

Roti: A Portable Feast

Originating from the Indian influence in the Caribbean, roti is a musttry for anyone visiting St. John. This wrap, filled with curried meats or vegetables, is both hearty and flavorful. Picture yourself biting into a warm, tender roti filled with succulent chicken or spicy chickpeas. It's the ultimate street food, perfect for those onthego moments between beach hopping and exploring.

Callaloo: The Caribbean Superfood

Callaloo is a nutritious and delicious green leafy vegetable, often cooked into a rich, savory stew. Blended with okra, onions, garlic, and sometimes salted meat or crab, callaloo is a powerhouse of flavor and nutrients. It's the kind of dish that makes you feel good about indulging in a second helping. Plus, it's a great conversation starter—how many people back home can say they've tried callaloo?

Fresh Seafood: Ocean to Table

With the Caribbean Sea at its doorstep, St. John boasts an impressive array of fresh seafood. From grilled mahimahi to buttery lobster tails, the island's seafood offerings are a testament to its rich maritime resources. Don't miss out on trying some local favorites like wahoo or snapper, often served with a side of rice and peas and a splash of lime.

Bush Tea: A Sip of Tradition

Bush tea is more than just a beverage; it's a taste of tradition. Made from local herbs and plants, each sip offers a soothing blend of flavors that are both refreshing and healthful. Whether you're starting your day with a cup or winding down in the evening, bush tea is a staple that connects you to the island's roots.

Tips for Enjoying Local Cuisine

- Embrace the Spice: Caribbean cuisine is known for its bold flavors. Don't shy away from trying dishes with a bit of heat—you might just discover a new favorite.
- Ask the Locals: The best recommendations often come from those who know the island best. Ask locals where they like to eat for an authentic culinary experience.
- Try Everything: Be adventurous with your palate. The diverse food scene in St. John means there's always something new and exciting to try.

Exploring the local specialties of St. John is like embarking on a culinary treasure hunt. Each dish tells a story, blending the island's cultural influences and natural bounty. So, grab your fork (or your hands, for those Johnny cakes) and dive into the delicious world of St. John's cuisine. Bon appétit!

Popular Restaurants

St. John's restaurant scene is as vibrant and diverse as its stunning landscapes. From beachside shacks to elegant dining rooms, the island offers a culinary experience that tantalizes every taste bud. Whether you're a foodie looking for the next great meal or just want to enjoy a lovely dinner with a view, here are some of the popular restaurants you must try in St. John.

1. ZoZo's at Caneel Bay

Location: North Shore Rd, Caneel Bay, St. John, USVI 00830

Phone: (860-977-6323

 ZoZo's at Caneel Bay is a fine dining restaurant offering Italian cuisine with a

Caribbean twist. Located in the historic ruins of an 18th-century sugar mill, it provides a romantic and unforgettable dining experience.

Unique Features:

- Historic Setting: Dine in the atmospheric ruins of a sugar mill.
- Ocean Views: Stunning views of the Caribbean Sea and neighboring islands.
- Signature Dishes: Fresh pasta, seafood, and delectable desserts.

- Wine Selection: Extensive wine list to complement the exquisite menu.

Hours:

- Dinner: 5:30 PM – 9:30 PM (Closed Tuesdays)

Price Range: $30 - $50 per entrée

Dining at ZoZo's feels like stepping into a postcard-perfect scene, where history and luxury blend seamlessly. The candlelit tables and ocean breeze create a magical ambiance that makes every meal feel like a special occasion.

2. **Morgan's Mango**

Location: Cruz Bay, St. John, USVI 00831

Phone: (340) 693-8141

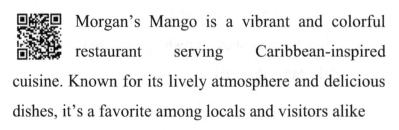 Morgan's Mango is a vibrant and colorful restaurant serving Caribbean-inspired cuisine. Known for its lively atmosphere and delicious dishes, it's a favorite among locals and visitors alike

Unique Features:

- Caribbean Flavors: Dishes infused with tropical flavors and fresh ingredients.
- Live Music: Regular live music performances add to the festive vibe.
- Signature Cocktails: A wide range of tropical cocktails to enjoy.
- OpenAir Dining: Breezy, openair seating perfect for enjoying the island atmosphere.

Hours:

- Dinner: 5:00 PM – 10:00 PM (Closed Sundays)

Price Range: $20 - $40 per entrée

Morgan's Mango is like a carnival for your taste buds. The lively music, colorful decor, and mouthwatering dishes make it a place where every meal feels like a celebration of island life.

3. **Extra Virgin Bistro**

Location: 1B Cruz Bay Quarter, Cruz Bay, St. John, USVI 00831

Phone: (340-715-1864)

Extra Virgin Bistro is a chic and modern restaurant focusing on farm-to-table dining. With a menu that changes based on seasonal availability, it offers fresh and innovative dishes.

Unique Features:

- FarmtoTable: Emphasis on locally sourced and seasonal ingredients.
- Creative Cuisine: Innovative dishes that blend Mediterranean and Caribbean flavors.
- Elegant Setting: Stylish decor and a relaxed, upscale atmosphere.

- Signature Cocktails: Craft cocktails made with fresh, local ingredients.

Hours:

- Dinner: 5:00 PM – 9:00 PM (Closed Sundays)

Price Range: $25 - $45 per entrée

Extra Virgin Bistro feels like a sophisticated culinary adventure. Every dish is a masterpiece, and the fresh, local flavors will make your taste buds dance with joy. It's a place where you can indulge in gourmet dining without any pretense.

4. The Longboard

Location: 2C Cruz Bay Quarter, Cruz Bay, St. John, USVI 00831

Phone: (340) 715-2210

The Longboard is a trendy restaurant and bar offering a fusion of Caribbean and coastal cuisine. With its laid-back vibe and delicious menu, it's the perfect spot for a casual yet memorable meal.

Unique Features:

- Coastal Cuisine: A menu inspired by the flavors of the Caribbean and coastal regions.
- Craft Cocktails: Refreshing cocktails featuring fresh, local ingredients.
- Casual Atmosphere: Relaxed, beachy decor and friendly service.
- Small Plates: Perfect for sharing and sampling a variety of flavors.

Hours:

- Lunch and Dinner: 11:30 AM – 10:00 PM

Price Range: $15 - $30 per entrée

The Longboard feels like a cool ocean breeze on a hot day. It's the kind of place where you can kick back, sip a tropical cocktail, and enjoy a delicious meal without a care in the world. Every bite is a little taste of paradise.

5. The Terrace Restaurant

Location: Wharfside Village, Cruz Bay, St. John, USVI 00831

Phone: (340) 779-8550

The Terrace Restaurant offers French-inspired cuisine with a Caribbean twist. With its elegant waterfront setting and sophisticated menu, it's a top choice for fine dining in Cruz Bay.

Unique Features:

- Waterfront Dining: Stunning views of Cruz Bay and the harbor.
- FrenchCaribbean Cuisine: A menu that combines French techniques with Caribbean flavors.
- Romantic Ambiance: Elegant decor and intimate seating.
- Extensive Wine List: Carefully curated wine selection to complement the menu.

Hours:

- Dinner: 5:30 PM – 9:30 PM (Closed Mondays)

Price Range: $30 - $50 per entrée

Dining at The Terrace feels like a romantic escape to a French bistro by the sea. The sophisticated flavors and beautiful views create a dining experience that's both elegant and enchanting. It's the perfect place to savor the finer things in life.

6. **Rhumb Lines**

Location: 3 Estate Emmaus, Coral Bay, St John 00830, US Virgin Islands

Phone: (340) 776-0303

Rhumb Lines is an eclectic restaurant serving a fusion of Asian and Caribbean cuisine. Known for its unique flavors and cozy setting, it's a hidden gem in Cruz Bay.

Unique Features:

- Fusion Cuisine: A menu blending Asian and Caribbean flavors.
- Cozy Ambiance: Intimate setting with warm, inviting decor.
- Signature Dishes: Popular dishes like Thai curry and jerk chicken.
- Friendly Service: Attentive and welcoming staff.

Hours:

- Dinner: 5:30 PM – 9:30 PM (Closed Tuesdays)

Price Range: $20 - $40 per entrée

Rhumb Lines feels like a culinary adventure around the world. The exotic flavors and cozy atmosphere make it a perfect spot for a relaxed and flavorful dining experience. It's a place where you can savor the spice of life in every bite.

These popular restaurants in St. John offer a diverse array of dining experiences, from fine dining to casual eateries, each with its unique charm and delicious flavors. Enjoy your culinary journey on this beautiful island!

MustSee Attractions

Beaches

St. John's beaches are the stuff of dreams—pristine stretches of sand, crystal-clear waters, and a backdrop of lush greenery that make you feel like you've stepped into a postcard. Whether you're a sunbather, snorkeler, or beachcomber, the island's beaches offer something for everyone. Let's dive into some of the must-see sandy paradises that St. John has to offer.

1. **Trunk Bay**

Location: North Shore Rd, St. John, USVI 00830

Phone: (340) 776-6201 (Virgin Islands National Park)

 Trunk Bay is often regarded as one of the most beautiful beaches in the world. Known for its pristine white sand, crystal-clear waters, and vibrant underwater snorkeling trail, it's a paradise for beachgoers and snorkel enthusiasts.

Unique Features:

- Underwater Snorkel Trail: A marked trail with signs providing information about the marine life.
- Facilities: Showers, restrooms, and a snack bar.
- Lifeguards: On duty during peak hours for added safety.

- Scenic Beauty: Stunning views of surrounding cays and lush hillsides.

Hours:

- Beach Access: 8:00 AM – 4:00 PM

Price Range:

Entrance Fee: $5 per person (Free for children under 16)

Trunk Bay feels like stepping into a dream. The soft sand, gentle waves, and colorful fish create a surreal experience that makes you feel like you're swimming in an aquarium. It's the kind of beauty that stays with you long after you've left the shore.

2. **Cinnamon Bay**

Location: North Shore Rd, St. John, USVI 00830

Phone: (340) 776-6201 (Virgin Islands National Park)

Cinnamon Bay is one of the longest beaches on St. John, offering ample space for sunbathing, swimming, and exploring. Its tranquil waters and extensive amenities make it a perfect destination for families and adventure seekers.

Unique Features:

- Water Sports: Equipment rentals for kayaking, paddleboarding, and snorkeling.
- Camping: Adjacent campground for those who want to stay close to nature.
- Facilities: Restrooms, showers, and a small store.
- Historical Ruins: Nearby sugar mill ruins add a touch of history to your visit.

Hours:

- Beach Access: 8:00 AM – 4:00 PM

Price Range:

Entrance Fee: Free (Camping fees vary)

Cinnamon Bay feels like an endless stretch of paradise. Whether you're paddling on the calm waters or exploring the historical ruins, there's a sense of peace and adventure that makes every moment memorable.

3. **Maho Bay**

Location: North Shore Rd, St. John, USVI 00830

Phone: (340) 776-6201 (Virgin Islands National Park)

Maho Bay is a favorite for its calm, shallow waters and abundant marine life. It's the ideal spot for families with young children and anyone looking to snorkel with sea turtles.

Unique Features:

- Sea Turtles: Frequent sightings of turtles feeding on seagrass close to shore.
- Beach Bar: Maho Crossroads offers drinks, snacks, and live music.
- Shallow Waters: Gentle entry makes it safe for children and novice swimmers.
- Picnic Area: Shaded picnic tables for a relaxing beachside meal.

Hours:

- Beach Access: 8:00 AM – 4:00 PM

Price Range:

- Entrance Fee: Free

Maho Bay feels like a warm embrace from nature. Watching the sea turtles glide through the water and enjoying a cold drink at the beach bar, you'll feel a sense of pure joy and relaxation that only a perfect beach day can bring.

4. <u>Hawksnest Beach</u>

Location: North Shore Rd, St. John, USVI 00830

Phone: (340) 776-6201 (Virgin Islands National Park)

Hawksnest Beach is a popular spot for its convenient location and beautiful coral reefs. It's a great place for snorkeling, picnicking, and soaking up the sun.

Unique Features:

- Coral Reefs: Excellent snorkeling just off the shore.
- Picnic Facilities: Covered picnic tables and BBQ grills.
- Shade: Plenty of trees providing natural shade.
- Easy Access: Close to Cruz Bay with ample parking.

Hours:

- Beach Access: 8:00 AM – 4:00 PM

Price Range:

Entrance Fee: Free

94

Hawksnest Beach feels like your own private escape. With its easy access and serene environment, it's the perfect spot to unwind, snorkel among vibrant coral reefs, and enjoy a leisurely picnic under the trees.

5. <u>Salt Pond Bay</u>

Location: South Shore Rd, St. John, USVI 00830

Phone: (340) 776-6201 (Virgin Islands National Park)

Salt Pond Bay is a hidden gem on the quieter side of St. John. Known for its excellent snorkeling and scenic hiking trails, it offers a more secluded and adventurous beach experience.

Unique Features:

- Snorkeling: Clear waters with diverse marine life, including rays and colorful fish.
- Hiking Trails: Trails leading to Ram Head and Drunk Bay for stunning views.
- Seclusion: Less crowded, providing a peaceful atmosphere.
- Salt Pond: Nearby salt pond adds an interesting element to the landscape.

Hours:

- Beach Access: 8:00 AM – 4:00 PM

Price Range:

- Entrance Fee: Free

Salt Pond Bay feels like a secret paradise. The combination of pristine beach, excellent snorkeling, and scenic hikes makes it a haven for those seeking tranquility and adventure away from the crowds.

These must-see beaches in St. John each offer something unique, ensuring that every beach lover can find their perfect slice of paradise on this beautiful island. Enjoy your beach-hopping adventure!

Virgin Islands National Park: A Tropical Paradise

Virgin Islands National Park, located on the island of St. John, is a stunning gem in the Caribbean. Covering approximately 60% of the island, this park is a sanctuary of natural beauty and cultural history. With its lush tropical forests, pristine beaches, and rich marine life, the park offers a diverse range of ecosystems and a myriad of activities for visitors to enjoy. Established in 1956, it protects over 7,000 acres of land and 5,500 acres of adjacent marine habitats, ensuring that the island's natural and historical treasures remain unspoiled for generations to come.

What to Expect?

When visiting Virgin Islands National Park, prepare to be awed by its sheer beauty and tranquility. Here's a glimpse of what awaits you:

1. **Beaches and Bays**: The park boasts some of the most breathtaking beaches in the world. Trunk Bay, with its underwater snorkeling trail, is a must-visit for both novice and experienced snorkelers. Cinnamon

Bay offers a more relaxed atmosphere with options for windsurfing and kayaking. Maho Bay is perfect for those looking to swim with sea turtles in their natural habitat.

2. **Hiking Trails**: The park features over 20 miles of hiking trails that wind through tropical forests, past historic ruins, and up to scenic overlooks. Popular trails include the Reef Bay Trail, which takes you past ancient petroglyphs and the ruins of a sugar mill, and the Ram Head Trail, offering stunning views of the coastline.

3. **Wildlife**: The park is home to a diverse range of wildlife. You can spot iguanas, mongoose, and a variety of bird species in the forested areas. The surrounding waters are teeming with marine life, including colorful fish, sea turtles, and rays.

4. Historical Sites: Explore the remnants of the island's colonial past, including sugar plantation ruins, petroglyphs carved by the Taino people, and historic Danish buildings. The Annaberg Plantation offers a glimpse into the island's sugar-producing history with well-preserved ruins and informative displays.

5. **Water Activities**: Snorkeling, diving, and kayaking are popular activities within the park. The clear, warm waters provide excellent visibility for underwater exploration, revealing vibrant coral reefs and an abundance of marine life.

Hours and Visitor Information

The park is open year-round, but here are some key details to help you plan your visit:

Visitor Center: The main visitor center is located in Cruz Bay and is open daily from 8:00 AM to 4:30 PM. Here, you can get maps, brochures, and information about guided tours and ranger-led programs.

Entrance Fees: As of 2024, there is no entrance fee to the park itself, but certain activities and sites, like Trunk Bay, may have fees for amenities and services. It's always a good idea to check the latest updates on the park's official website or at the visitor center.

Guided Tours and Programs: The park offers a variety of ranger-led tours and educational programs. These include guided hikes, snorkeling tours, and cultural demonstrations. These programs are an excellent way to gain deeper insight into the park's natural and historical significance.

Tips for Your Visit

- Start Early: To make the most of your day and avoid the midday heat, start your visit early in the morning.

- Bring Essentials: Pack plenty of water, sunscreen, insect repellent, and snacks. Many trails and beaches are remote, and facilities may be limited.

- Respect Nature: Help preserve the park's beauty by following Leave No Trace principles. Stay on designated trails, do not disturb wildlife, and take your trash with you.

Snorkel Gear: Bring your own snorkel gear if you plan to explore the underwater trails. Rentals are available, but having your own ensures a better fit and comfort.

- Weather: Keep an eye on the weather, especially during hurricane season (June to November). Check for any advisories or park closures before heading out.

Visiting Virgin Islands National Park is like stepping into a natural paradise where every turn offers a new adventure. Whether you're hiking through verdant trails, exploring underwater wonders, or soaking up the sun on a pristine beach, this park is sure to leave you with unforgettable memories. So lace up your hiking boots, grab your snorkel gear, and get ready to explore the natural wonders of St. John!

Historical Sites in St. John

St. John, with its rich and varied history, offers numerous historical sites that provide a fascinating glimpse into the island's past. From ancient indigenous carvings to colonial-era ruins, these sites are a testament to the island's cultural heritage and historical significance. Here's a detailed guide to some of the must-see historical sites on St. John.

Annaberg Sugar Plantation

The Annaberg Sugar Plantation is one of the most well-preserved and informative historical sites on St. John. This former sugar plantation offers a vivid look into the island's colonial history and the sugar industry's impact on its development.

What to Expect:

- Ruins: Explore the remains of the windmill, factory, and slave quarters. The structures provide a stark reminder of the harsh conditions endured by the enslaved people who worked here.

- Educational Displays: Informative plaques and displays throughout the site offer insights into the sugar production process and the plantation's history.
- Scenic Views: The site offers stunning views of the surrounding area, making it a picturesque spot for history and nature enthusiasts alike.

Hours and Visitor Information:

- Open Daily: The site is open from sunrise to sunset.
- Admission: Free, though donations to help preserve the site are appreciated.
- Guided Tours: Rangerled tours are available, providing deeper insights into the history of the plantation.

Catherineberg Ruins

 Nestled within the Virgin Islands National Park, the Catherineberg Ruins are the remnants of a 18th-century sugar plantation. This less-visited site offers a peaceful and reflective experience.

What to Expect:

- Ruins: The site features the remains of the windmill and other plantation structures. The windmill, in particular, is wellpreserved and offers a glimpse into the engineering of the time.

- Serenity: Unlike more popular sites, Catherineberg is often less crowded, providing a tranquil setting to ponder the island's past. Most Taxis don't even like passing through that route so its better you use your own transportation or try if you can get a taxi to take you there.

Hours and Visitor Information:

- Open Daily: The site is accessible from sunrise to sunset.
- Admission: Free.
- No Facilities: There are no facilities on-site, so plan accordingly.

Reef Bay Trail Petroglyphs

The Reef Bay Trail is a scenic hike that leads to ancient petroglyphs carved by the Taino people, the island's indigenous inhabitants. These petroglyphs are a significant archaeological and cultural site.

What to Expect:

- Hiking: The trail is moderately challenging, with a descent into the valley leading to the petroglyphs. The hike is approximately 2.2 miles each way.

- Petroglyphs: The petroglyphs are carved into rocks near a freshwater pool, depicting various symbols and figures. They offer a fascinating glimpse into the spiritual and cultural practices of the Taino people.
- Sugar Mill Ruins: Continue along the trail to discover the ruins of the Reef Bay Sugar Mill, adding another layer of historical intrigue to your hike.

Hours and Visitor Information:

- Open Daily: The trail is accessible from sunrise to sunset.
- Guided Hikes: The National Park Service offers guided hikes that include transportation back to the starting point. Reservations are recommended.

Fortsberg

Fortsberg is a historic fort site with roots dating back to the 18th century. It played a significant role in the island's colonial defenses and was the site of a notable slave rebellion in 1733.

What to Expect:

- Ruins: The fort's remnants include the walls and foundation of the structure. The site offers commanding views of Coral Bay and the surrounding areas.
- Historical Significance: Informative plaques detail the fort's history and the 1733 slave rebellion, providing context to the ruins.

Hours and Visitor Information:

- Open Daily: Accessible from sunrise to sunset.
- Admission: Free.
- Hiking Required: Reaching the fort involves a moderate hike, so wear appropriate footwear and bring water.

Estate Concordia Ruins

Located near the Concordia Eco-Resort, these ruins are remnants of another 18th-century sugar plantation. The site is less developed but offers an intriguing look at the island's colonial history.

What to Expect:

- Ruins: Explore the scattered remains of the plantation buildings, including the great house and sugar mill.
- Views: The site offers beautiful views of the surrounding area, combining historical exploration with natural beauty.

Hours and Visitor Information:

- Open Daily: Accessible from sunrise to sunset.
- Admission: Free.
- SelfGuided Exploration: There are no formal tours, so you can explore at your own pace.

Tips for Visiting Historical Sites

- Wear Comfortable Shoes: Many sites involve hiking or walking on uneven terrain. Sturdy, comfortable shoes are a must.

- Bring Water and Snacks: Facilities are limited at many sites, so come prepared.

- Respect the Sites: These locations are of great historical and cultural importance. Treat them with respect by not touching or climbing on the ruins.

- Check for Updates: Hours and availability can change, especially due to weather or maintenance. Check the National Park Service website or local sources for the latest information.

Exploring the historical sites of St. John is a journey through time, offering insights into the island's complex past and the people who have shaped it. Each site provides a unique perspective, making your visit to

St. John not only a tropical getaway but also an enriching historical experience.

Museums and Cultural Centers in St. John

St. John offers a variety of museums and cultural centers that provide deep insights into the island's rich history, vibrant culture, and unique heritage. Here's a comprehensive guide to some of the must-visit museums and cultural centers on St. John, complete with up-to-date information for 2024.

Elaine Ione Sprauve Library and Museum

The Elaine Ione Sprauve Library and Museum, located in the Enighed Estate House, is a cultural treasure trove. It houses a collection of historical artifacts, photographs, and documents that chronicle the history and culture of St. John.

What to Expect:

- Historical Artifacts: The museum's exhibits include artifacts from the island's colonial period, including tools, household items, and relics from the sugar plantation era.
- Photographs and Documents: Extensive collections of photographs and historical documents provide a visual and narrative history of the island.
- Library: The library offers a selection of books, periodicals, and research materials related to the Caribbean and Virgin Islands history and culture.

Hours and Visitor Information:

- Open Monday to Friday: 9:00 AM to 5:00 PM.
- Admission: Free, though donations are appreciated.

- Guided Tours: Available upon request, providing deeper insights into the exhibits.

Bajo El Sol Gallery and Art Bar

 Bajo El Sol Gallery and Art Bar, located in Mongoose Junction, is a vibrant cultural center that showcases contemporary

Caribbean art. It serves as both an art gallery and a cultural hub, promoting the work of local artists and offering a space for creative expression.

What to Expect:

- Art Exhibits: Rotating exhibits feature works by local artists, including paintings, sculptures, and mixedmedia pieces. The gallery highlights contemporary Caribbean art and traditional crafts.
- Cultural Events: The gallery hosts regular events, including art openings, live music performances, and artist talks. These events provide a lively atmosphere and an opportunity to engage with the local art scene.
- Art Bar: The Art Bar offers a selection of drinks and a cozy space to relax and enjoy the artworks.

Hours and Visitor Information:

- Open Daily: 10:00 AM to 7:00 PM.

Admission: Free, though purchasing art or drinks supports local artists.

Special Events: Check their website or social media for upcoming events and exhibits.

<u>St. John School of the Arts</u>

Phone: +1 340-779-4322

Location: 86H4+X8J St John, Frank St, Cruz Bay, St John 00830,

 The St. John School of the Arts is a cultural institution dedicated to fostering artistic education and appreciation. It offers classes, workshops, and performances in various art forms, including music, dance, theater, and visual arts.

What to Expect:

- Classes and Workshops: The school offers a range of classes for all ages and skill levels. From dance and music to visual arts and theater, there's something for everyone interested in exploring their creative side.

- Performances: Regular performances and recitals showcase the talents of students and visiting artists. These events are a great way to experience the local arts scene.

- Community Programs: The school is committed to community outreach, offering programs and scholarships to make the arts accessible to all residents and visitors.

Hours and Visitor Information:

- Open Monday to Friday: 9:00 AM to 5:00 PM, with additional hours for events and classes.

- Admission: Varies by class and event; some community programs are free.

- Event Calendar: Check their website for the latest schedule of classes, workshops, and performances.

The Gifft Hill School - Education and Cultural Programs

Phone: +1 340-776-1730

Location: 86JH+C69, Rte 104, Cruz Bay, St John 00830,

The Gifft Hill School is not only an educational institution but also a center for cultural enrichment on St. John. The school hosts various programs and events that celebrate the island's cultural heritage and promote community engagement.

What to Expect:

- Cultural Events: The school organizes events such as cultural fairs, art shows, and musical performances that highlight the diverse cultural traditions of St. John.
- Educational Programs: Programs are designed to educate both students and the community about the island's history, ecology, and cultural practices.
- Community Involvement: The school actively involves the community in its programs, fostering a sense of shared cultural identity and heritage.

Hours and Visitor Information:

- School Hours: Monday to Friday, 8:00 AM to 3:00 PM.
- Event Admission: Varies; many events are free or lowcost.

- Program Information: Visit their website or contact the school for details on upcoming events and programs.

Exploring the museums and cultural centers of St. John offers a deep dive into the island's rich heritage, vibrant arts scene, and enduring traditions. Whether you're an art lover, history buff, or curious traveler, these sites provide a meaningful and enriching experience.

Suggested Itineraries

One-day visit itinerary(essential sights)

Here's a detailed one-day visit itinerary for St. John, USVI, for 2024. This itinerary includes a mix of beaches, historical sites, and local dining to give you a well-rounded experience of the island.

One-Day Visit Itinerary in St. John, USVI

7:30 AM – Arrival in Cruz Bay

Start your day by arriving in Cruz Bay, the main port of entry for St. John. If you're coming from St. Thomas, take the ferry which offers a scenic ride.

Unique Features: Beautiful views of the surrounding islands during the ferry ride.

The excitement of arriving at a new destination sets the tone for an adventure-filled day.

123

8:00 AM – Breakfast at Sun Dog Café

Location: Mongoose Junction, Cruz Bay, St. John, USVI 00830

Phone: (340) 693-8340

Enjoy a delicious breakfast at Sun Dog Café, known for its vibrant atmosphere and great vegetarian options.

Hours: 8:00 AM – 9:00 PM

Price Range: $10 - $25 per entrée

Unique Features: Live music and outdoor seating in a charming courtyard.

Savor a hearty breakfast while basking in the morning sun and the lively ambiance of Mongoose Junction.

9:00 AM – Visit Trunk Bay

Location: North Shore Rd, St. John, USVI 00830

Phone: (340) 776-6201 (Virgin Islands National Park)

Head to Trunk Bay, one of the most beautiful beaches in the world, famous for its underwater snorkel trail.

Hours: 8:00 AM – 4:00 PM

Price Range: $5 per person (Free for children under 16)

Unique Features: Pristine white sand, crystal-clear waters, and a marked underwater snorkel trail.

Dive into the clear waters and explore the vibrant marine life, feeling like you're swimming in an underwater paradise.

11:00 AM – Explore Annaberg Sugar Plantation

Location: Annaberg Rd, St. John, USVI 00830

Phone: (340) 776-6201 (Virgin Islands National Park)

Visit the historic Annaberg Sugar Plantation ruins and learn about the island's sugar production history.

Hours: 9:00 AM – 4:00 PM

Price Range: Free

Unique Features: Well-preserved ruins and informative signage.

Walk through history and imagine the lives of those who worked on the plantation, gaining a deeper understanding of the island's past.

12:30 PM – Lunch at The Longboard

Location: 2C Cruz Bay Quarter, Cruz Bay, St. John, USVI 00831

Phone: (340) 715-2210

Enjoy a delicious lunch at The Longboard, offering a fusion of Caribbean and coastal cuisine with great vegetarian options.

Hours: 11:30 AM – 10:00 PM

Price Range: $15 - $30 per entrée

Unique Features: Fresh, local ingredients and a casual, beachy atmosphere.

Relish the flavors of the Caribbean while relaxing in a cool, laid-back setting.

2:00 PM – Relax at Maho Bay

Location: North Shore Rd, St. John, USVI 00830

Phone: (340) 776-6201 (Virgin Islands National Park)

Spend the afternoon at Maho Bay, a tranquil beach known for its calm waters and frequent sea turtle sightings.

Hours: 8:00 AM – 4:00 PM

Price Range: Free

Unique Features: Shallow waters, sea turtle sightings, and a nearby beach bar.

Feel a sense of wonder as you watch sea turtles swim gracefully through the clear waters.

4:00 PM – Shopping at Mongoose Junction

- Location: Mongoose Junction, Cruz Bay, St. John, USVI 00830

Head back to Cruz Bay and explore the shops at Mongoose Junction, where you can find unique souvenirs and local crafts.

- Unique Features: A variety of shops offering handmade jewelry, art, and clothing.

Enjoy a leisurely shopping experience, picking up keepsakes that will remind you of your beautiful day on St. John.

5:30 PM – Dinner at Morgan's Mango

Location: Cruz Bay, St. John, USVI 00831

Phone: (340) 693-8141

End your day with a delightful dinner at Morgan's Mango, offering Caribbean-inspired cuisine in a vibrant setting.

Hours: 5:00 PM – 10:00 PM (Closed Sundays)

Price Range: $20 - $40 per entrée

Unique Features: Live music and a festive atmosphere.

Savor the rich flavors and lively ambiance, celebrating a day well spent on this beautiful island.

8:00 PM – Departure from Cruz Bay

Catch the ferry back to St. Thomas, reflecting on your wonderful day in St. John.

Unique Features: Scenic evening ferry ride with views of the island lights.

As the ferry departs, feel a sense of fulfillment and happiness from your adventure, looking forward to your next visit.

This one-day itinerary offers a perfect blend of relaxation, exploration, and local cuisine, ensuring you experience the best of St. John in just one day. Enjoy your trip!

Weekend Getaway Itinerary for St. John, USVI

Friday: Arrival and Exploration

Morning:

- 8:00 AM: Arrival at Cruz Bay via ferry from St. Thomas.

 - Tip: Grab a coffee and breakfast at **North Shore Deli (located in Mongoose Junction)**. Enjoy their fresh pastries and breakfast sandwiches.

Mid-Morning:

- 9:30 AM: Check-in at your hotel.

 - Luxury Option: **Caneel Bay Resort** - Enjoy beachfront rooms and unparalleled service.

- Mid-Range Option: **St. John Inn** - A charming, affordable stay with a pool and complimentary breakfast.

- Budget Option: **Cruz Bay Boutique Hotel** - Cozy rooms in the heart of Cruz Bay.

Late Morning:

- 10:30 AM: Head to **Trunk Bay Beach.**

- Famous for its underwater snorkeling trail. Rent snorkeling gear at the beach.

- Tip: Get there early to avoid the crowds and secure a good spot on the beach.

Afternoon:

- 12:30 PM: Lunch at **High Tide Bar & Seafood Grill**.

- Located in Cruz Bay, offering fresh seafood and stunning views of the bay.

- Recommendation: Try the fish tacos or the lobster roll.

Mid-Afternoon:

- 2:00 PM: Visit the **Virgin Islands National Park Visitor Center**.

  - Learn about the island's history, flora, and fauna.

  - Tip: Join a guided tour or pick up a map for hiking trails.

Late Afternoon:

- 4:00 PM: Short hike to **Honeymoon Beach.**

  - Enjoy water activities like kayaking and paddleboarding. Equipment can be rented on-site.

Evening:

- 6:00 PM: Return to your hotel to freshen up.

Night:

- 7:30 PM: Dinner at **Morgan's Mango**.

  - A lively spot offering Caribbean cuisine with a focus on fresh, local ingredients.

  - Recommendation: Try the conch fritters and the grilled mahi-mahi.

Saturday: Adventure and Relaxation

Morning:

- 7:00 AM: Early breakfast at your hotel or at **Sun Dog Cafe** in Mongoose Junction.

  - Known for their hearty breakfast options and relaxed atmosphere.

Mid-Morning:

- 8:30 AM: Head out for a day trip to the Coral Bay area.

- Stop 1: **Reef Bay Trail Hike**.

- A moderate hike leading to the petroglyphs and a waterfall.

- Tip: Bring plenty of water and wear sturdy shoes.

Late Morning:

- 11:30 AM: Explore **Salt Pond Bay**.

- Ideal for snorkeling and spotting sea turtles.

- Tip: Pack a picnic lunch to enjoy on the beach.

Afternoon:

- 1:00 PM: Lunch **at Miss Lucy's** in Coral Bay.

- Famous for their island-style dishes and waterfront dining.

- Recommendation: Try the goat curry or the vegetarian platter.

Mid-Afternoon:

- 2:30 PM: Relax and swim at **Maho Bay Beach**.

- Calm waters, great for swimming and paddleboarding.

- Tip: Keep an eye out for sea turtles and rays in the shallow waters.

Evening:

- 5:00 PM: Return to Cruz Bay.

Night:

- 6:30 PM: Sunset sail from Cruz Bay.

- Option: **Kekoa Sailing Expeditions** - Offers a relaxing sail with stunning sunset views.

- Tip: Book in advance to secure your spot.

Late Night:

- 8:30 PM: Dinner at The **Terrace**.

  - Upscale dining with a focus on fresh seafood and gourmet dishes.

  - Recommendation: The catch of the day and their extensive wine list.

Sunday: Leisure and Departure

Morning:

- 7:30 AM: Breakfast at The **Longboard**.

  - Casual spot known for its fresh, healthy breakfast options.

  - Recommendation: Try the avocado toast or the acai bowl.

Mid-Morning:

- 9:00 AM: Relax at **Cinnamon Bay Beach**.

- One of the largest beaches on the island, perfect for a leisurely morning.

- Tip: Rent a lounge chair and umbrella for ultimate relaxation.

Late Morning:

- 11:00 AM: Explore the nearby **Cinnamon Bay Plantation Ruins**.

- A short walk from the beach, offering a glimpse into the island's history.

Afternoon:

- 12:30 PM: Light lunch at Cruz Bay Landing.

- Known for their sandwiches and refreshing drinks.

- Recommendation: The chicken Caesar wrap and a tropical smoothie.

Early Afternoon:

- 2:00 PM: Last-minute shopping in Cruz Bay.

  - Check out Mongoose Junction for unique souvenirs and local crafts.

Late Afternoon:

- 4:00 PM: Head back to the ferry terminal for your departure to St. Thomas.

Evening:

- 6:00 PM: Ferry ride to St. Thomas and onward travel.

Enjoy your weekend getaway to St. John, USVI! Each day is packed with a mix of adventure, relaxation, and delicious food, ensuring a memorable and rejuvenating experience.

Shopping in St John

Souvenir Shops

When visiting St. John, taking a piece of this island paradise back home is a must, and the vibrant souvenir shops scattered around the island offer just the right mementos to cherish your trip. From locally crafted jewelry to handmade soaps, these shops provide a treasure trove of unique items that reflect the island's culture, beauty, and artisanal spirit.

Mongoose Junction

Mongoose Junction is a charming shopping complex in Cruz Bay, and it's a top spot for finding high-quality, unique souvenirs. The blend of Caribbean architecture and lush gardens makes shopping here a delightful experience.

Highlights:

- Bajo El Sol Gallery: This gallery features stunning artworks by local artists, including paintings, ceramics, and prints. Purchasing a piece here not only brings home a beautiful memory but also supports the local art community.
- The Friends of Virgin Islands National Park Store: Offering a variety of eco-friendly and educational products, this shop is perfect for nature lovers. You'll find books, apparel, and gifts that celebrate the island's natural beauty and help support conservation efforts.

Wharfside Village

Located right along the waterfront in Cruz Bay, Wharfside Village combines shopping with scenic ocean views. It's an ideal spot to find a range of souvenirs while enjoying the sea breeze.

Highlights:

- Bamboula: This shop is known for its colorful Caribbeanthemed items. From vibrant clothing and accessories to home decor and handcrafted gifts, Bamboula captures the essence of island life.
- Sugar Birds: A boutique offering an array of unique jewelry, pottery, and art. Each piece is carefully selected to represent the local culture and craftsmanship.

Coral Bay

For those venturing to the quieter side of the island, Coral Bay offers some hidden gems when it comes to souvenir shopping. This area is perfect for finding unique, handmade items in a more laid-back setting.

Highlights:

- Jolly Dog Trading Company: Known for its eclectic mix of merchandise, Jolly Dog offers everything from tshirts and hats to handmade jewelry and islandinspired art. It's a onestop shop for quirky and memorable gifts.

- Pickles in Paradise: While primarily a deli and bar, Pickles in Paradise also features a small selection of local crafts and souvenirs. Enjoy a meal or drink while browsing their unique offerings.

Local Craft Markets

Don't miss the opportunity to visit local craft markets, where you can meet artisans and purchase directly from the makers. These markets are often vibrant with local culture and provide a unique shopping experience.

Highlights:

- Caribbean Craft Fair: Held periodically in Cruz Bay, this fair features a variety of local vendors selling handmade crafts, jewelry, art, and more.

It's a great place to find oneofakind items and support local artisans.

- Farmer's Market: In addition to fresh produce, the farmer's market in Coral Bay often has stalls with locally made goods, including soaps, candles, and other handcrafted items.

Tips for Souvenir Shopping

Look for Local: Prioritize buying items made by local artisans. Not only does this support the community, but it also ensures your souvenirs are authentic and unique.

Ask Questions: Don't hesitate to ask shop owners or artisans about the story behind their products. Knowing the history or inspiration behind an item adds to its sentimental value.

Respect Customs: If purchasing items made from natural materials, be aware of customs regulations to avoid any issues when taking your souvenirs home.

Shopping for souvenirs on St. John is more than just a retail experience; it's an opportunity to connect with the island's culture, support local artisans, and take home a piece of the paradise you've enjoyed. Whether you're browsing charming boutiques or exploring lively markets, each purchase carries the spirit of St. John and the memories of your tropical adventure.

Events and Festivals

Annual Events

St. John, with its vibrant culture and close-knit community, hosts a variety of annual events that offer visitors a unique glimpse into the island's heart and soul. Each event is more than just a celebration; it's a testament to the island's rich heritage, love for music, and deep-rooted traditions. Here's a look at some of the most cherished annual events that you simply can't miss.

St. John Carnival (June-July)

The St. John Carnival, often considered the highlight of the island's social calendar, is a month-long festival of music, dance, and color. Held in late June and early July, this event culminates in a grand parade on the Fourth of July.

What to Expect:

- Parades and Pageants: The streets come alive with vibrant parades, featuring elaborately costumed dancers, steel bands, and floats. The pageantry is a feast for the eyes and a true celebration of Caribbean culture.

- Music and Dancing: Calypso, reggae, and soca rhythms fill the air as live bands perform throughout the festivities. You'll find yourself irresistibly drawn into the joyful, infectious beat.

- Cultural Exhibits: Local artisans showcase their crafts, offering handmade jewelry, art, and traditional foods. It's a great opportunity to support local creators and take home unique souvenirs.

Love City Live! (January)

Love City Live! is a reggae and soul music festival that brings together renowned artists and enthusiastic crowds in the serene setting of St. John. Held annually in January, this event is perfect for music lovers seeking to start the year with soulful tunes and good vibes.

What to Expect:

- Concerts: Enjoy performances by top reggae and soul musicians against the backdrop of the Caribbean Sea. The concerts are held at picturesque locations, making for an unforgettable experience.
- Beach Parties: The festival includes lively beach parties where you can dance barefoot in the sand, meet new friends, and soak in the laid-back island atmosphere.

- Cultural Activities: Beyond the music, the festival offers cultural workshops and activities, providing a deeper connection to the island's heritage.

Thanksgiving Regatta (November)

The Thanksgiving Regatta, held in late November, is a beloved event that brings together sailors and spectators for a weekend of competitive racing and camaraderie.

What to Expect:

- Sailing Races: Watch as sleek sailboats race across the azure waters, showcasing the skills and sportsmanship of local and visiting sailors. The sight of colorful sails against the blue sky is simply mesmerizing.
- Community Events: The regatta is more than just a sporting event; it's a community gathering. Enjoy barbecues, live music, and

social events that bring together locals and visitors alike.

- Family-Friendly Activities: With activities for all ages, including kids' games and educational exhibits about marine life, the regatta is a perfect family outing.

St. John Blues Festival (March)

For blues enthusiasts, the St. John Blues Festival in March is a must-attend event. This festival attracts top blues musicians from around the world, offering an immersive experience of soulful music in a tropical paradise.

What to Expect:

- Live Performances: Enjoy electrifying performances by acclaimed blues artists in intimate, scenic venues. The music resonates through the island, creating an atmosphere of shared passion and enjoyment.

- Workshops and Jam Sessions: Participate in workshops led by the artists themselves, and join in impromptu jam sessions that capture the true spirit of the blues.

- Island Hospitality: The festival also highlights the warm hospitality of St. John, with local restaurants and bars offering special menus and events in conjunction with the festival.

These annual events are more than just dates on a calendar; they are the heartbeat of St. John. They bring together locals and visitors, fostering a sense of community and belonging. The laughter, music, and shared experiences create lasting memories, making every moment on this island unforgettable. Whether you're swaying to the rhythms of reggae, cheering at a sailboat race, or exploring local crafts, each event offers a chance to connect deeply with the island's culture and its people. So, mark your calendar and join in the celebrations—you'll leave with not just souvenirs, but stories and friendships that last a lifetime.

Practical Information

Currency and Banking

Navigating the financial landscape of a new destination can often feel daunting, but in St. John, it's surprisingly straightforward, making your trip all the more enjoyable. Here's what you need to know about currency and banking on this beautiful island, infused with a touch of local charm and warmth.

Currency

U.S. Dollar (USD): The official currency of St. John is the U.S. dollar, making it convenient for American visitors. No need to worry about currency exchanges or fluctuating rates—your dollars will work just fine here.

Cash is King: While credit and debit cards are widely accepted, especially in Cruz Bay and at most hotels, restaurants, and larger shops, it's always a good idea to carry some cash. Many smaller vendors, particularly those at local markets and some eateries in Coral Bay, may prefer cash transactions. Plus, there's something nostalgic and comforting about paying in cash at a charming local stand, interacting directly with the friendly islanders.

ATMs and Banks

ATMs: You'll find several ATMs conveniently located around St. John, primarily in Cruz Bay. Major banks like Scotiabank have branches with ATMs that accept a wide range of cards. These ATMs dispense U.S. dollars, and using them is as straightforward as back home. Remember, though, that ATM fees can add up, so it might be wise to withdraw larger amounts at once.

Banking Hours: Banks on St. John typically operate from Monday to Friday, with hours generally running from 9 a.m. to 4 p.m. It's good to note that banks may close for lunch, so planning your visit accordingly can save you a wait.

Credit Cards: Most establishments accept major credit cards, such as Visa, MasterCard, and American Express. However, always double-check, especially in smaller or more remote spots. It's a bit like a treasure hunt, discovering the places where your plastic might not be as welcome.

Practical Tips

Currency Exchange: If you're arriving from outside the U.S., you might need to exchange your currency. While there aren't many dedicated currency exchange services on the island, banks can usually assist.

Additionally, some hotels offer currency exchange, though the rates might not be as favorable.

Tipping: Tipping is customary and appreciated in St. John, much like in the mainland U.S. A standard tip of 15-20% in restaurants, bars, and for services like taxis is common. It's a small way to show gratitude for the warm hospitality you'll receive.

Budgeting: While St. John can cater to both luxury travelers and those on a budget, having a financial plan can enhance your experience. It's easy to get swept up in the island's allure, from dining at exquisite waterfront restaurants to purchasing beautiful handcrafted souvenirs. A little financial foresight ensures you can enjoy all that St. John offers without any stress.

Handling money matters on vacation often feels like a chore, but in St. John, it's part of the adventure. Every transaction, from withdrawing cash at a bustling ATM in Cruz Bay to tipping a friendly taxi driver, connects you to the island and its people. It's these small interactions that make your visit personal and memorable.

St. John's straightforward banking system and familiar currency provide a sense of ease and comfort, allowing you to focus on what truly matters—enjoying the island's breathtaking beauty and warm community. As you explore, dine, and shop, each exchange becomes a piece of your travel story, a reminder that sometimes, the simplest aspects of travel are the most enriching.

Health and Safety and Emergency Contacts

Traveling to a tropical paradise like St. John is an exhilarating adventure, but it's essential to be prepared for the unexpected. Understanding the health and safety protocols, as well as knowing the emergency contacts, ensures a worry-free and enjoyable stay. Here's everything you need to know to keep your trip as smooth as the island's serene beaches.

Health and Safety

Medical Facilities: While St. John is a small island, it is well-equipped to handle medical emergencies. The Myrah Keating Smith Community Health Center, affiliated with the Schneider Regional Medical Center on nearby St. Thomas, offers comprehensive care for both residents and visitors. It's comforting to know that in case of illness or injury, professional medical help is just a short drive away.

Pharmacies: There are several pharmacies in Cruz Bay where you can get over-the-counter medications, prescriptions, and basic first aid supplies. It's always a good idea to carry any specific medications you need and ensure they are in their original, labeled containers.

Travel Insurance: Investing in travel insurance that covers health emergencies is a wise decision. It provides peace of mind, ensuring that you are protected against unexpected medical expenses, allowing you to focus on creating unforgettable memories.

Health Tips:

- Hydration and Sun Protection: The Caribbean sun can be intense. Stay hydrated and use sunscreen with a high SPF to protect your skin. Wearing a hat and sunglasses adds an extra layer of protection.

- Insect Repellent: Mosquitoes and other insects are common, especially in lush areas. Pack and use insect repellent to avoid bites and potential diseases like dengue fever.

- Local Cuisine: While the food in St. John is delicious, your stomach might need some time to adjust. Eat at reputable places and start with smaller portions to gauge your tolerance.

Safety Precautions

General Safety: St. John is known for its friendly atmosphere and low crime rate. However, practicing common-sense precautions like not leaving valuables unattended on the beach or in your car, and being mindful of your surroundings, ensures a safe experience.

Water Safety: The island's beaches are stunning, but ocean currents can be strong. Pay attention to local advisories and flags indicating water conditions. Snorkeling and swimming are best enjoyed with a buddy for added safety.

Emergency Contacts

Knowing who to call in an emergency can be a lifesaver. Here are the crucial contacts you should keep handy:

Police, Fire, Ambulance: Dial 911 for any emergency. This central number connects you to all necessary emergency services.

Myrah Keating Smith Community Health Center: (340) 693-8900. This facility provides urgent and routine medical care.

Schneider Regional Medical Center (St. Thomas): (340) 776-8311. For more serious health issues, this hospital is a short ferry ride away.

Poison Control Center: (800) 222-1222. For any concerns regarding poisoning or hazardous substance exposure.

Coast Guard: (340) 776-3497. For emergencies at sea or related to water activities.

Traveling is about immersing yourself in new experiences, and peace of mind plays a crucial role in that. Knowing that St. John has robust health and safety measures in place allows you to relax and fully embrace the island's charm. Whether you're basking in the sun, exploring lush trails, or enjoying a night out, these precautions and contacts ensure that help is readily available should you need it.

Remember, every adventure carries some risks, but being prepared transforms potential worries into a sense of security. This way, you can focus on the joys of your journey—making memories, forging connections, and soaking in the beauty that is St. John. With your health and safety taken care of, all that's left is to enjoy every moment of your island escape.

Conclusion

As we reach the end of this comprehensive guide to St. John, let's take a moment to reflect on the enchanting journey we've mapped out. From the lush trails of Virgin Islands National Park to the serene, sun-drenched beaches, every chapter of this guide has been crafted to ensure you experience the very best of this tropical paradise.

We've delved into the vibrant history and modern charm of St. John, a place where the past and present coexist in a harmonious dance. You've discovered the best times to visit, ensuring you catch the island at its most magical moments, whether it's during the lively carnival season or the tranquil off-peak months. Our detailed packing tips and travel essentials have prepared you for every scenario, making sure you're ready to embrace all the adventures that await.

Getting to St. John has been simplified, with detailed information on air travel and ferry options. Once on the island, the guide has navigated you through public transportation, walking, and hiking routes, ensuring you can explore every corner with ease. We've introduced you to the island's culinary delights, from local specialties to popular restaurants, satisfying your taste buds with every bite.

The must-see attractions, including the pristine beaches and the awe-inspiring Virgin Islands National Park, have been highlighted to ensure you don't miss out on any of the island's wonders. For the history enthusiasts, we've unearthed the rich stories behind the island's historical sites and cultural centers. Shopping and annual events have been covered too, giving you a taste of local life and traditions.

Your health and safety are paramount, and we've provided up-to-date information on medical facilities, emergency contacts, and practical tips to ensure your peace of mind. Whether it's understanding the local currency and banking or knowing the best ways to stay safe while exploring, you're well-equipped to navigate any situation.

Now, as you prepare to embark on your St. John adventure, we encourage you to share your experiences. Your feedback is invaluable, and we'd love to hear how this guide has helped shape your journey. Did you find a hidden gem we missed? Did the packing tips save the day? Your insights will not only help us improve but also assist future travelers in discovering the magic of St. John.

We hope this guide has inspired you to explore, connect, and immerse yourself in all that St. John has to offer. The island is waiting, with its warm sunsets, friendly locals, and endless adventures. So, pack your bags, set your spirit free, and let St. John captivate your heart as it has ours.

Thank you for choosing this guide as your travel companion. We wish you safe travels, unforgettable experiences, and memories that will last a lifetime. And remember, we're just a review away from hearing all about your incredible journey. Happy travels!

Made in the USA
Middletown, DE
25 August 2024

59681217R10096